Dress Your Dog

Nifty Knits for Classy Canines

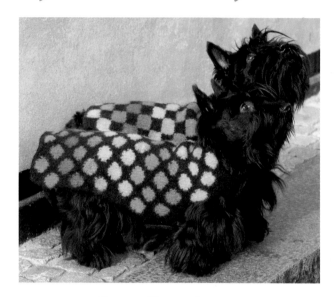

Sys Fredens

Martingale®
& COMPANY

D1122236

Dress Your Dog:
Nifty Knits for Classy Canines
© 2009 by Sys Fredens

Martingale & Company
19021 120th Ave. NE, Suite 102
Bothell, WA 98011-9511 USA
ShopMartingale.com

Printed in China
17 16 15 14   11 10 9 8 7 6

**Library of Congress Cataloging-in-Publication Data
is available upon request.**

ISBN: 978-1-56477-928-1

Hundestrik
Copyright text © Sys Fredens
Copyright photos © Claus Dalby
Publisher's Editor: Merete Kjær Christenson
Copyright © 2007 Forlaget Klematis A/S Publishers, Denmark
(www.klematis.dk)
This edition is published by arrangement with Claudia Böhme Rights & Literary Agency, Hannover, Germany (www.agency-boehme.com).

CREDITS

President & CEO • Tom Wierzbicki

Editor in Chief • Mary V. Green

Managing Editor • Tina Cook

Developmental Editor • Karen Costello Soltys

Translator • Carol Huebscher Rhoades

Technical Editor • Ursula Reikes

Copy Editor • Marcy Heffernan

Design Director • Stan Green

Production Manager • Regina Girard

Illustrator • Laurel Strand

Cover & Text Designer • Regina Girard

MISSION STATEMENT

*Dedicated to providing quality products
and service to inspire creativity.*

DOGS IN THE BOOK

Pages 8, 11, and 16: Caddy, Chihuahua

Pages 12, 19, and 20: Rocky, papillon

Page 15: Albert, Chihuahua

Pages 22 and 51: Freja, Kromfohrländer

Pages 23, 25, 26, 29, 30, 33, 34, 36, 37, 52, 54, 56, 57, and 58:
Kiko, West Highland white terrier

Pages 7, 38, 45, 46, and 49:
Esmeralda and Cirkeline, Scottish terriers

Page 42: Lizzie, Pembroke Welsh corgi

Pages 40 and 41: Anton and Victor, King poodles

acknowledgments

Thank you to all the dogs who were models for this book and who happily modeled all the new clothes and accessories. Of course a big thank you is in order for all the dog owners:

To my friends, Birthe and Kaare, for loaning Kiko, a West Highland white terrier and always a sweet little boarder.

To Anné and Flemming, for Lizzie, a sweet Pembroke Welsh corgi.

To my neighbor Maria, for letting me use her papillon, Rocky— he has such cute big ears.

To Tina Andrea for Albert, the fine Chihuahua, and Åse for Freja, a yellow Kromfohrländer (a very cheeky dog), all of whom I met on the street.

To Susanne, who owns a shop that sells dog accessories, and her beautiful Scottish terriers, Esmeralda and Cirkeline.

To Claus, who offered the two lovely King poodles, Anton and Victor.

Special thanks to Karin Jakobsen from Kennel Chihuahua Specials, who came with her daughter, Katja, and the sweetest little Chihuahua puppy, Caddy.

I'd also like to thank my daughter, Thit, who has been such a great inspiration, as she was for all of my earlier books.

contents

28 knitted flowers

31 ribbed wraparound vest

32 felted bag

35 ribbed knit with roll collar

36 cabled sweater with roll collar

39 raglan sweater

40 bandana

40 chew ring

43 zippered coat

44 norwegian sweater

47 overcoat with spots or blocks

49 knitted collar and leash

50 crocheted jacket with collar

52 rug with burgundy square

53 striped food mat

55 patchwork blanket

56 round crocheted pillow

59 square knitted pillow

Knitting for dogs is more popular than ever before. It began, as do so many other trends, in the United States, but has now come to Denmark. We've become more and more absorbed in our house pets; they are part of the family and must have the best. Suddenly there are shops just for animals, something we hadn't seen before. When you look at the choices of pet products, you have to ask—are these for the enjoyment of the animals or their humans? We must admit that, for the most part, they are for our enjoyment and the fantasy world we create. When it comes down to it, the dogs don't care if they sleep in an old basket with a rug or in a bed that looks like it was designed by Le Corbusier.

Entertainment value versus practicality is a bit different when it comes to dog clothes because, the fact is, many little dogs need clothes, especially the short-haired ones, so that they won't freeze when they are outside. Knitwear is a great choice for these clothes. Some knitted items are warm, some are fun to dress them in, and some resemble the stylish designs seen in glossy advertisements. You can also play with designs that suit both "mother" and "child"; for example, leg warmers can match the dog's coat. In that case, the practical is combined with the whimsical.

The photos in this book show a number of small dogs, for I am of the opinion that it is primarily these dogs that need protective garments. Larger dogs often look silly in a sweater or other clothing and would not, for anything in the world, laugh about it.

This book features patterns for smart, practical, romantic, and fun tops, sweaters, shrugs, coats, and more. You'll also find collars, leashes, and flowers (both knitted and crocheted) to embellish the garments. Finally, there are some lovely pillows and rugs that your dog can relax on.

Best wishes,
Sys Fredens

MATERIALS

50 g; 109 yds of medium-weight mohair in red plus a small amount of pink (**4**)

Crochet hook: Size J/10 (6 mm)

Side-release buckle, 1½" wide

Tapestry needle

INSTRUCTIONS

Collar

Turn and ch 1 at end of every row.

With red, ch 7, sc in second ch from hook and in each ch. Work in sc until collar measures 15¾".

With pink, work 1 row sc all around edge of collar.

Sew one end of collar securely to latch on side-release buckle and the other end to the clasp.

Pompon

Cut out two circles of heavy paper, 6" in diameter. Cut a 2½"-diameter circle from the center of the circles. Cut a small wedge from both circles to make it easy to wrap the yarn. Wrap both red and pink yarn around the template. Pull a strand through the yarn around the inner edge and tighten. Cut the yarn between the two layers of paper around the outer edge and trim evenly if necessary. Sew the pompon securely to collar clasp.

"I love going to the café with you, because I get to wear my pompon collar."

vest WITH ties

SIZES

XS (S, M)

FINISHED MEASUREMENTS

Circumference: 12 (16, 19½)"

Length: 8 (9¾, 11¾)"

MATERIALS

A   50 (100, 100) g; 88 (176, 176) yds of bulky-weight cotton/acrylic blend (**5**)

B   50 g; 65 yds of bulky-weight polyamide/metallic ribbon for tie (**5**)

Needles: Size 10 (6 mm) or size required for gauge

Crochet hook: Size J/10 (6 mm) for tie

1 stitch holder

GAUGE

14 sts and 30 rows = 4" in garter st with A

INSTRUCTIONS

Back and stomach: With A, CO 30 (40, 50) sts and work in garter st, inc 1 st at each side on EOR until there are a total of 42 (56, 70) sts. Knit without further incs until piece measures 4¾ (5, 7)".

Back: K6 (8, 10) and put these sts on holder, BO 5 (6, 7) sts, work until 11 (14, 17) sts rem; turn and knit over the center 20 (28, 36) sts until piece measures 7¾ (9½, 11½)" from beg CO.

Row of holes on back: K2 (1, 2), BO 1 st, [K3 (3, 4), BO 1 st] a total of 3 (5, 5) times, end with K1 (0, 2). On the next row, CO 1 st over each BO st. Knit 1 row and then BO.

Stomach: With RS facing you, attach yarn on left-hand edge at beg of back. BO 5 (6, 7) sts and work across to last 6 (8, 10) sts on needle, sl 6 (8, 10) sts from holder onto needle and knit the stomach over 12 (16, 20) sts until piece measures 7¾ (9½, 11½)" from beg CO.

Row of holes on front of neck: Work (K2, BO 1 st) until 3 sts rem, BO 1 st, K1. On the next row, CO 1 st over each BO st. Knit 1 row and then BO.

Finishing: Sew the edges of the stomach tog.

Tie: With B, make a crochet ch 27½ (31½, 35½)" long. Beg at center back, pull the tie through the holes on half of the back, through the holes in the front of neck, and through the other half of the holes on the back. Sew the tie securely to each side of the neck so that it won't twist.

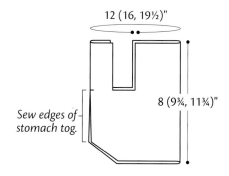

12 (16, 19½)"

8 (9¾, 11¾)"

Sew edges of stomach tog.

leg warmers FOR THE dog owner

FINISHED MEASUREMENTS

Circumference: 12"

Length: 8½"

MATERIALS

A   100 g; 176 yds of bulky-weight cotton/acrylic blend ⑤

B   50 g; 65 yds of bulky-weight polyamide/metallic ribbon for tie ⑤

Needles: Size 10 (6 mm) or size required for gauge

Crochet hook: Size J/10 (6 mm) for tie

GAUGE

14 sts and 30 rows = 4" in garter st

INSTRUCTIONS

With A, CO 42 sts and work in garter st until piece measures 6½".

Row of holes: K2, BO 1 st, (K5, BO 1 st) a total of 5 times. On next row, CO 1 st over each BO st. Knit 5 rows and then BO.

Sew the sides tog.

Tie: With B, crochet a ch about 27½" long. Beg at center front, pull the tie through the row of holes all around, ending at center front.

Make the other leg warmer the same way.

colorful coat

SIZES

S (M, L)

FINISHED MEASUREMENTS

Width: 11 (15, 18½)"

Length: 11¾ (15¾, 19¾)"

MATERIALS

1 (2, 2) skeins of Silk Garden from Noro (45% silk, 45% kid mohair, 10% wool; 50g; 109 yds) (**4**)

Needles: 10 (6 mm) or size required for gauge

2 buttons, approx 1" diameter

GAUGE

15 sts and 21 rows = 4" in St st

INSTRUCTIONS

Back: CO 27 (39, 51) sts and knit 1 row.

Next row: K3, inc 1, knit to last 3 sts, inc 1, K3.

Knit 1 row.

Keeping K3 at each edge, work in St st and inc as follows.

Row 1 (RS): Knit.

Row 2 and all WS rows: K3, purl to last 3 sts, K3.

Row 3: K3, inc 1, knit to last 3 sts, inc 1, K3.

Row 5: As row 1.

Row 7: As row 3.

Row 8: As row 2.

Work rows 1–8, inc on every 4th row until there are a total of 43 (57, 71) sts.

Work even until piece measures 6 (7, 8¾)", ending with a WS row.

Stomach strap: CO 22 sts using cable CO (see page 60) at right-hand edge—65 (79, 93) sts. Work the 22 sts in garter st and rem sts in St st for 4 (6, 8) rows.

First buttonhole: Work to last 4 sts, YO, K2tog, K2.

Work 5 (7, 9) rows.

BO 22 sts for strap and then work 1 row.

Beg decs on every other RS row as follows: K3, sl1-K1-psso, knit to last 5 sts, K2tog, K3.

Cont in St st working decs on EOR until 25 (39, 49) sts rem.

Neckband: CO 16 sts at right-hand edge—41 (55, 65) sts. Work the 16 sts in garter st and rem sts in St st for 4 (6, 8) rows.

Second buttonhole: Work to last 4 sts , YO, K2tog, K2.

Work 5 (7, 9) rows and BO all sts.

Finishing: Sew buttons onto straps so that straps fit well around the dog's stomach and neck.

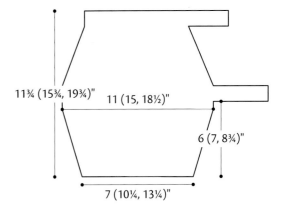

11¾ (15¾, 19¾)"
11 (15, 18½)"
6 (7, 8¾)"
7 (10¼, 13¼)"

ribbed sweater

SIZES

XXS (XS, S)

FINISHED MEASUREMENTS

Circumference: 10¼ (11¾, 14¼)"

Length: 9¾ (11¾, 13¾)" excluding roll collar

MATERIALS

1 (1, 2) skeins of Silk Garden from Noro (45% silk, 45% kid mohair, 10% wool; 50 g; 109 yds)

Needles: Size 9 (5.5 mm) or size required for gauge

GAUGE

18 sts and 28 rows = 4" in ribbing

RIBBING

Row 1 (WS): P1, (K1, P1) across.

Rows 2, 3, and 4: Knit the knit sts and purl the purl sts as they face you.

Row 5: K1 (P1, K1) across.

Rows 6, 7, and 8: Knit the knit sts and purl the purl sts as they face you.

Rep these 8 rows throughout.

INSTRUCTIONS

Body: CO 27 (29, 31) sts and work in ribbing, AT THE SAME TIME inc 1 st at each side on every 4th row 3 (4, 5) times—33 (37, 41) sts.

CO 3 (4, 5) at beg of next 4 rows—45 (53, 61) sts.

Work even until piece measures 6¼ (7, 8)".

Leg openings: Cont in ribbing, work 8 sts; turn and work 4 rows over these 8 sts. Cut yarn. BO next 6 (6, 8) sts. Work 17 (25, 29) sts; turn and work 4 rows over these sts. Cut yarn. BO next 6 (6, 8) sts. Work last 8 sts; turn and work 4 rows over these sts.

Joining row: Cont in ribbing, work 8 sts, CO 4 (4, 6) sts, work to next leg opening, CO 4 (4, 6) sts, finish row—41 (49, 57) sts.

Cont in ribbing, but K2tog twice over each leg opening on every 4th row 2 times—33 (41, 49) sts.

Work even until piece measures 9¾ (10¾, 11½)".

Roll collar: Work in ribbing for 1½ (1½, 2¼)" and BO in ribbing.

Finishing: Sew sides of stomach and collar tog. Fold down collar on RS.

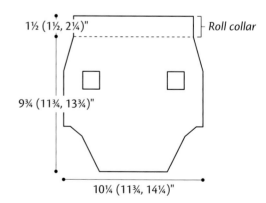

"My sweater is knit in a colorful wool yarn, and the ribbing makes it fit perfectly."

"After a walk in the woods, it's nice to have a bag ready so I can rest my tired little legs."

crocheted shoulder bag

MEASUREMENTS BEFORE FELTING

Circumference: 34"

Height at back: 10¼"

Height at front: 8¼"

MATERIALS

5 skeins of Kureyon from Noro (100% wool; 50 g; 109 yds)

Crochet hook: Size J/10 (6 mm) or size required for gauge

Afghan hook: Size K/10½ (6.5 mm)

GAUGE BEFORE FELTING

12 sts and 13 rnds = 4" with size J/10 hook

14 sts and 24 rows = 4" with size K/10½ hook

INSTRUCTIONS

Base (sc in rnd): With size J/10 hook, ch 8 and join into a ring with 1 sl st, ch 1. Work in the rnd and finish each rnd with 1 sl st in ch 1 of previous rnd, and beg next rnd with ch 1.

Rnd 1: Sc 16 into ring.

Rnd 2: (Sc 1, 2 sc in next st) around—24 sts.

Rnd 3: (Sc 2, 2 sc in next st) around—32 sts.

Rnd 4: (Sc 3, 2 sc in next st) around—40 sts.

Cont incs in this manner, working 1 more sc between incs (inc should be stacked one over the other) until 9 rnds have been worked—80 sts.

Crochet 1 rnd even.

Now work incs on every other rnd until there are a total of 19 rnds—120 sts. The base should measure approx 11¾" in diameter. Fasten off.

Bag (Tunisian crochet—see page 22): With size K/10½ afghan hook, ch 120 and work in Tunisian crochet until side measures 8¼".

First strap: Work in Tunisian crochet over first 30 sts for 2". Cut yarn. Sk first 16 sts (from side seam), join yarn and work in Tunisian crochet over rem 14 sts until strap measures approx 15¾". Fasten off.

Second strap: Sk 60 sts from first strap, join yarn and work last 30 sts in Tunisian crochet for 2". Work over first 14 sts only until strap measures approx 15¾". Fasten off.

Finishing: Sew side seams of bag. Sew end of straps tog. Work 1 row sc with size J/10 hook along edge of bag and strap. Crochet base and bag's lower edge tog.

Felting: Machine wash bag in hot water with a little soap. Check progress often and remove when desired size. Shape bag before drying and let dry completely.

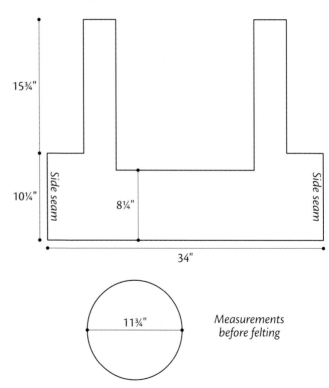

Measurements before felting

striped crocheted top

SIZES

S (M, L)

FINISHED MEASUREMENTS

Circumference: 16 (19, 22)"

Length: 7 (9½, 11¾)" excluding roll collar

MATERIALS

Worsted-weight superwash wool 〔4〕

   50 (50, 100) g; 125 (125, 250) yds in color Blue

   50 (50, 100) g; 125 (125, 250) yds in color Beige

Crochet hooks: Size G/6 (4 mm) and H/8 (5 mm) or size required for gauge

4 stitch markers

GAUGE

18 sts and 19 rows = 4" with smaller hook

Pattern

Work all sc through back loops only so the RS will have ridges.

Stripes

Alternate 5 rnds of blue and 5 rnds of beige throughout. When changing colors, work a sl st with the old color and ch st in the new color.

Join each rnd with a slip st into ch of previous rnd and beg rnd with ch 1.

INSTRUCTIONS

Body: With smaller hook and beige, ch 72 (86, 100) and join into a ring with a sl st, ch 1.

Work 1 rnd in single crochet. Work 4 rnds in patt.

Change colors and work alternating stripes in patt until piece measures 3½ (5¼, 6¾)".

Leg openings: Pm, ch 8 (10, 12) for leg, pm, sk 10 (12, 14) sts for leg, sc 39 (46, 54) for back, pm, ch 8 (10, 12) for leg, pm, sk 10 (12, 14) sts for leg, sc 13 (16, 18) for stomach—68 (82, 96) sts. On next rnd, sc in back loop of each st and in each ch.

Cont in patt, dec 1 st at each side of back and stomach on every 4th rnd until 56 (66, 76) sts rem.

Work even until piece measures 7 (9½, 11¾)".

Roll collar: Turn piece wrong side out and work in patt with beige and larger hook until collar measures 1¼ (1½, 2)".

Leg bands: With RS facing you, join blue yarn at beg of the 8 (10, 12) sts of leg opening, work 1 rnd in patt with inc as follows: *sc 2 in first ch, sc in next 6 (8, 10) chs, sc 2 in last ch, sc 10 (12, 14)—20 (24, 28) sts. Work even in patt for 2 (3, 4) rnds. Work other leg the same way.

Finishing: Fold down collar on RS.

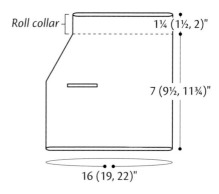

Roll collar — 1¼ (1½, 2)"

7 (9½, 11¾)"

16 (19, 22)"

SIZES

S (M, L)

FINISHED MEASUREMENTS

Circumference: 16 (19½, 23½)"

Length: 11½ (15, 19)"

MATERIALS

150 (250, 350) g; 375 (625, 875) yds of light worsted-weight superwash wool (3)

Needles: Size 6 (4 mm) straight and size 6 (4 mm) double-pointed needles (or 2 circular needles) or size required for gauge

Cable needle

1 stitch marker

2 stitch holders

GAUGE

34 sts and 31 rows = 4" in cable patt

CABLE PATTERN

3/3CF: Sl 3 sts to cn and hold at front, K3, K3 from cn.

Rows 1 and 5 (RS): P2, *K6, P1; rep from * to last 8 sts, K6, P2.

Rows 2 and 4: K2, *P6, K1; rep from * to last 8 sts, P6, K2.

Row 3: P2, *3/3CF, P1; rep from * to last 8 sts, 3/3CF, P2.

Row 6: As row 2.

Rep rows 1–6.

INSTRUCTIONS

Back: CO 101 (129, 157) sts, and set up cable patt on WS as follows: K2, *P6, K1; rep from * to last 8 sts, P6, K2. Work cable patt and AT THE SAME TIME inc 1 st at each side on next RS row, and on every 4th row for a total of 5 times; work incs into patt—111 (139, 167) sts.

Cont until cable has been crossed 4 (6, 8) times, and then work 1 row.

Body: CO 22 (29, 36) sts at end of row, divide sts onto dpns (or 2 circulars) to work in the rnd—133 (168, 203) sts. Pm at left side of CO sts to mark beg of rnd. Work in cable patt over all sts until there are 9 (13, 17) cable crossings total. Cut yarn.

Leg openings: Place first 13 (13, 20) sts on holder for leg, join yarn and work 6 cable rows over next 85 (113, 127) sts for back. Cut yarn. Place next 13 (13, 20) sts on a holder for leg, join yarn and work 6 cable rows over next 22 (29, 36) sts for stomach.

Work cable patt on all sts and CO 6 (6, 13) sts over sts on holders—119 (154, 189) sts. Cont in cable patt, dec 1 st over each leg opening on every other rnd 7 times—105 (140, 175) sts.

Work without further shaping until there are 5 (6, 7) cable crossings above leg openings. Work 1 rnd and then BO kw.

Leg bands: With RS facing you, place sts from holder on needle, PU 6 sts along side of leg, 6 (6, 13) sts along CO row and 6 sts on other side of leg—31 (31, 45) sts. Work in St st for ¾". BO kw. Work other leg the same way.

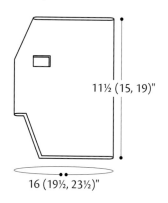

11½ (15, 19)"

16 (19½, 23½)"

MATERIALS

50 g; 65 yds of bulky-weight polyester ribbon yarn (**5**)

Crochet hook: Size J/10 (6 mm)

Afghan hook: Size J/10 (6 mm)

Carabiner hook, ¾" diameter

⅝"-wide purchased collar

Sharp needle and sewing thread

TUNISIAN CROCHET

Always crochet with RS facing; do not turn work.

Ch the required number of sts and turn with ch 1.

Row 1: Insert hook into top loop of second ch from hook, yarn over hook and pull through; leave loop on hook. *Insert hook into next ch, yarn around hook and pull through; leave loop on hook; rep from * for each ch across.

Row 2 (return row—worked from left to right): *Yarn around hook and pull through first 2 loops on hook; rep from * across. Now only 1 st remains on hook.

Row 3 (forward row—worked from right to left): *Insert hook under first vertical thread of a st (do not work into first vertical thread below the hook), yarn around hook and pull through a loop; rep from * across, keeping all loops on hook, to last vertical thread. Insert hook under both vertical threads at the end, yarn around hook and pull through a loop.

Rep rows 2 and 3.

INSTRUCTIONS

Leash

With afghan hook, ch 115 and work 6 rows Tunisian crochet (end with a completed return row).

Work 1 row sc.

Fold one end down 8" for handhold and sew securely. Sew carabiner hook to other end.

Collar

With crochet hook, ch 93. Dc in third ch from hook and in each ch. Insert the purchased collar in and out of double crochet sts. Sew ends securely on each side.

crocheted leash AND collar

MATERIALS

50 g; 65 yds of bulky-weight cotton/acrylic yarn (**5**)

Crochet hook: Size H/8 (5 mm)

59" length of nylon band ⅝" wide for the leash

Carabiner hook, ¾" in diameter

Belt buckle with ¾" inner measurement for collar

INSTRUCTIONS

Leash

Ch 182. Dc in second ch from hook and in each ch. Turn and ch 1.

Sc in each dc, working through front loops only. Turn and ch 2.

Dc in each sc. Turn and ch 1.

Fold the leash lengthwise and crochet it tog with sc.

Pull nylon band through the leash.

Fold one end down 8" for handhold and sew securely. Sew carabiner hook to other end.

Collar

Ch 4. Sc in second ch from hook and each sc—3 sts. Turn and ch 1.

Work in sc for ¾". Inc 1 st at each side—5 sc.

Cont in sc until piece measures about 21" or desired length. If desired, taper end by working sc2tog, sc, sc2tog, then 2 more rows in sc. Cut yarn.

Fold the 3-st end around the belt buckle and sew securely to WS.

Loop

Join yarn with sc to edge about ¾" from buckle, work ch st for 1¼", and sew securely to edge on opposite side.

shrug

SIZES

S (M, L)

FINISHED MEASUREMENTS

Length from cuff to cuff: 10½ (14, 22)"

Width: 7 (8, 9½)"

MATERIALS

50 g; 150 yds of light worsted-weight mohair blend

Needles: Size 8 (5 mm) and 10½ (6.5 mm) or size required for gauge

Crochet hook: Size J/10 (6 mm)

3 stitch markers

GAUGE

14 sts and 18 rows = 4" on larger needles

INSTRUCTIONS

First cuff: With smaller needles, CO 21 (25, 29) sts and work in K1, P1 ribbing for 2¾".

Body: Change to larger needles and St st, and inc 1 st at each side on EOR twice—25 (29, 33) sts. Pm at each side.

Cont in St st until St st portion measures 5¼ (7, 11)". Pm to indicate center back.

Work second half of body until length is same as center back to last inc on first half. Dec 1 st at each side on EOR twice—21 (25, 29) sts.

Second cuff: Change to smaller needles and work in K1, P1 ribbing for 2¾". BO in ribbing.

Finishing: Stitch sides of cuff tog.

Work 1 row sc, and 1 row crab st (see page 60) along both edges of body between cuffs.

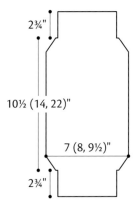

2¾"

10½ (14, 22)"

7 (8, 9½)"

2¾"

"Please notice my pink lace dress. I love to wear it when we walk in town."

lace dress

SIZES

S (M, L)

FINISHED MEASUREMENTS

Circumference: 15 (19½, 24½)"

Length: 9½ (10¼, 11½)" excluding roll collar

MATERIALS

100 (150, 150) g; 250 (375, 375) yds of light worsted-weight superwash wool (**3**)

Needles: Set of size 6 (4 mm) double-pointed needles or size required for gauge

1 stitch marker

2 stitch holders

GAUGE

19 sts and 36 rnds = 4" in lace patt

Lace Pattern (worked in the round)

Rnd 1: (K2tog) 2 times, *(YO, K1) 4 times, (K2tog) 4 times; rep from * to last 8 sts, (YO, K1) 4 times, (K2tog) 2 times.

Rnds 2 and 3: Knit.

Rnd 4: Purl.

Rep these 4 rnds.

INSTRUCTIONS

CO 72 (96, 120) sts, join, pm, and knit 1 rnd.

Work in lace patt until piece measures 5½ (6¼, 7)". End with rnd 1 of lace patt.

Back: Turn and work *back and forth* over next 36 (60, 72) sts in patt as follows.

Purl 1 row.

Knit 2 rows.

Work rnd 1 of lace patt.

Work these 4 rows a total of 2 times. Cut yarn.

Stomach: Working on rem 36 (36, 48) sts, place first 12 sts on a holder for leg opening, slip next 12 (12, 24) sts to right needle, turn, join yarn and work back and forth in patt for 8 rows. Make sure the patts on back and stomach match. Place rem 12 sts on a holder for leg opening. With 12 (12, 24) sts on RH needle, cont around and CO 10 sts with backward loop (see page 60) over leg opening, work back sts in patt, CO 10 sts for leg opening—68 (92, 116) sts.

Gusset: Join, pm, work stomach and back sts in lace patt, work 10 sts for leg openings in St st except for purl ridge, AT THE SAME TIME dec 1 st at each side of leg opening on every other rnd as follows. First dec rnd: ssk, K6, K2tog; next dec rnd: ssk, K4, K2tog. Cont dec as est until 1 leg st rem, work last st for each leg tog with st from back—48 (72, 96) sts.

Work without shaping in patt until piece measures 9½ (10¼, 11½)". End on rnd 1 of patt.

Knit 4 rnds.

Next rnd (inc): *K4 (6, 8), M1; rep from * around—60 (84, 108) sts.

Roll collar: Turn WS out, beg with rnd 3 of lace patt and work 12 rnds. BO loosely kw.

Leg bands: With RS facing you, PU 30 (34, 38) sts around leg opening and work 3 rnds in St st. Purl 1 rnd and then BO kw. Work other leg the same way.

Finishing: Fold down collar on RS.

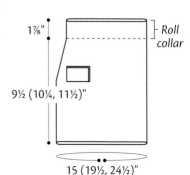

1⅞"

Roll collar

9½ (10¼, 11½)"

15 (19½, 24½)"

flowers

crocheted flowers

SIZE

S (M, L) depends on yarn and hook size used

MATERIALS

Crochet hook

Between 6 and 8 yards of yarn

Small: Size D/3 (3.25 mm) with sport-weight yarn

Medium: Size G/6 (4 mm) with light worsted-weight yarn

Large: Size H/8 (5 mm) with medium worsted-weight yarn

INSTRUCTIONS

Ch 26 (21, 16).

Row 1: Sc 2 in second ch from hook and in each ch. Turn with ch 1.

Row 2: Sc 1 in next sc, *ch 2, 1 sc in next st; rep from * across. Turn with ch 4.

Row 3: Sl st 1 in next loop, *ch 4, 1 sl st in next loop; rep from * across.

Roll flower tog lengthwise and sew along beg ch.

knitted flowers

SIZE

S (M, L) depends on yarn and needle size used

MATERIALS

Needles

Between 6 and 8 yards of yarn

Small: Size 3 (3.25 mm) with sport-weight yarn

Medium: Size 6 (4 mm) with light worsted-weight yarn

Large: Size 8 (5 mm) with medium worsted-weight yarn

INSTRUCTIONS

CO 25 (20, 16) sts.

Row 1: K1, (YO, K1) across.

Row 2: Purl.

Row 3: As for row 1.

Row 4: As for row 2.

Row 5: K2, BO 1, *(CO 1 st on right needle, BO) 3 times, K1tbl, BO; rep from * across.

Roll flower tog lengthwise and sew along CO row.

crocheted flowers

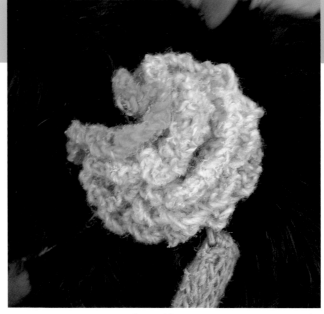

knitted flower

crocheted and knitted flowers

"I have no desire for a bone just now. I'd rather sit outside in my vest."

ribbed wraparound vest

SIZES

S (M, L)

FINISHED MEASUREMENTS

Width: 6¾ (8, 9½)" unstretched

Length: 19¾ (23¾, 27½)"

To fit circumference: 15¾ (19¾, 23¾)" when overlapped

MATERIALS

100 (150, 200) g; 250 (375, 500) yds of light worsted-weight superwash wool **3**

Needles: Size 6 (4 mm) or size required for gauge

Kilt pin

GAUGE

35 sts and 28 rows = 4" unstretched

INSTRUCTIONS

Back: CO 62 (70, 86) sts.

P2, (K2, P2) across. Cont in ribbing until piece measures 8¾ (10¾, 11¾)".

First leg opening: Work ribbing over 18 (22, 26) sts, BO 18 (18, 22) sts, finish row. On next row, work in ribbing and CO 18 (18, 22) sts using backward loop (see page 60) over BO sts.

Stomach: Work in ribbing for 3½ (3¾, 4½)".

Second leg opening: Work as for first leg opening.

Back: Work until piece measures 19¾ (23¾, 27½)". BO in ribbing.

Wrap vest around stomach, overlap on back to fit, and secure with a kilt pin.

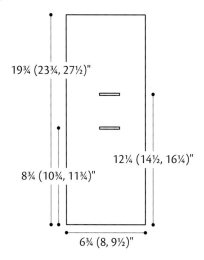

19¾ (23¾, 27½)"

12¼ (14½, 16¼)"

8¾ (10¾, 11¾)"

6¾ (8, 9½)"

felted bag

MEASUREMENTS BEFORE FELTING

Width: 20½"

Height: 10¾"

Depth: 7"

MATERIALS

600 g; 650 yds of bulky-weight wool **5**

Needles: Size 19 (15 mm) or size required for gauge

2 pieces of 1¼"-wide nylon band for handle, approx 52" each

Tapestry needle

Sharp needle and sewing thread to match nylon band

GAUGE

Before felting: 6½ sts and 11 rows = 4" with 2 strands of yarn held tog

INSTRUCTIONS

First section: With 2 strands of yarn held tog, CO 28 sts and purl 1 row. Beg incs as follows: K1, M1, knit to end.

Cont in St st, inc 1 st at beg on EOR until there are 34 sts.

Work 18 rows without shaping and end on a knit row.

Base: Knit 1 row, this is first ridge on RS.

Work 19 rows in St st, ending with a knit row.

Knit 1 row, this is second ridge on RS.

Second section: Work 18 rows in St st, ending on a purl row.

Dec 1 st at beg of row as follows: K1, sl1-K1-psso, knit to end. Dec on EOR until 28 sts rem. Purl 1 row and then BO kw.

The ends of the bag are different sizes and worked separately.

Short end: CO 15 sts and work 18 rows in St st. BO all sts.

Long end: CO 15 sts and work 30 rows in St st. BO all sts.

Finishing: Attach 7" side of short end to front (with the shaped corners) base section, and then attach each side of short end to side front edges. Attach long end the same way on opposite side.

Felting: Machine wash bag in hot water with a little soap. Check progress often and remove when desired size. Shape bag, making sure base is flat. Dry completely.

Handle: With sharp needle and sewing thread, beg 6" in from front edge of base, sew nylon band securely up side, leave about 23¾" free for handle, then with 3½" in between, sew band on same side, then across bottom of base, and up other side, leaving 23¾" free for handle, cont with 3½" in between and sew down side and finish at base where band first started.

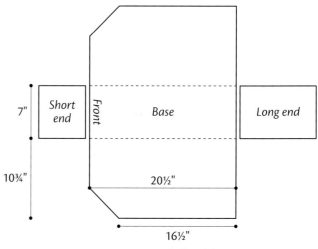

Measurements before felting

"When we are going on the bus, we always take this bag for me to sit in. The bag can also be folded down so I have my own basket."

ribbed knit WITH roll collar

SIZES

S (M, L)

FINISHED MEASUREMENTS

Circumference: 14 (16½, 20½)"

Length: 9 (10½, 12¼)" excluding roll collar

MATERIALS

150 (150, 200) g; 275 (275, 365) yds of bulky-weight superwash wool (**5**)

Needles: Set of size 10½ (6.5 mm) double-pointed needles or size required for gauge

1 stitch marker

2 stitch holders

GAUGE

21 sts and 21 rows = 4" in ribbing unstretched

INSTRUCTIONS

Sweater is worked from the collar down.

Roll collar: CO 52 (64, 76) sts; join, being careful not to twist sts, pm to indicate center. Work in K1, P1 ribbing for 2¾ (3¼, 3½). Note that knit st after marker is considered center st.

Inc rnds: Work to marker, inc 1, work center st, inc 1. Inc on every rnd in ribbing until there are 76 (92, 108) sts. Work incs into K1, P1 patt as much as possible.

Leg openings: Work to 11 (13, 15) sts after marker, turn and work 4 rows over next 21 (25, 29) sts. Cut yarn. Place next 7 (7, 9) sts on a holder. Join yarn and work 5 rows over next 41 (53, 61) sts. Place next 7 (7, 9) sts on a holder. CO 7 (7, 9) sts over the sts on holder, work to next st holder and CO 7 (7, 9) sts over the sts on holder—76 (92, 108) sts. Join into rnd, place another marker at beg of rnd.

Dec rnds: *Work to 2 sts before center marker, sl1-K1-psso, work center st, K2tog, finish rnd. Work 1 rnd. Work to 2 sts before center marker, P2tog, work center st, P2tog, finish rnd. Work 1 rnd.* Rep from * to * until 64 (78, 92) sts rem. Work decs into patt as much as possible.

Back: Work to 5 (6, 8) sts before center marker, BO next 9 (11, 15) sts. Work back and forth on rem sts, dec 1 st at each side on every other row until 41 (51, 59) sts rem. BO in ribbing.

Leg bands: Place sts from holder onto dpns and PU 17 (19, 21) sts around leg opening—24 (26, 30) sts. Work in ribbing for 2½ (2½, 2¾)" and BO in ribbing. Work other leg the same way.

Finishing: Fold down collar and fold up legs on RS.

2¾ (3¼, 3½)" — *Roll collar*

9 (10½, 12¼)"

14 (16½, 20½)"

cabled sweater WITH roll collar

SIZES

S (M, L)

FINISHED MEASUREMENTS

Circumference: 17½ (19½, 23)"

Length: 9½ (11¾, 13¾)" excluding roll collar

MATERIALS

200 g; 218 yds of bulky-weight wool (5)

Needles: Size 10½ (6.5 mm) straight and a set of size 10½ (6.5 mm) double-pointed needles or size required for gauge

Cable needle

1 stitch marker

GAUGE

15 sts and 20 rnds = 4" in patt

Cable Pattern

3/3CF: Sl 3 sts to cn and hold at front, K3, K3 from cn.

K1 in st below: See page 61.

Rows 1, 3, 5, and 7 (WS): K2, (P6, K2, P1, K2) a total of 2 (3, 4) times; end P6, K2.

Rows 2 and 6: P2, (K6, P2, K1 in st below, P2) a total of 2 (3, 4) times, K6, P2.

Row 4: P2, (3/3CF, P2, K1 in st below, P2) a total of 2 (3, 4) times, 3/3CF, P2.

Row 8: P2, (K6, P2, K1 in st below, P2) a total of 2 (3, 4) times, K6, P2.

Rep rows 1–8.

INSTRUCTIONS

Back: CO 32 (43, 54) sts and work rows 1 through 3 of cable patt. On 4th row of cable patt, inc 1 st at each side. Cont in cable patt,

inc 1 st at each side on every 2nd (4th, 4th) row twice—38 (49, 60) sts. Work without shaping until there are 2 (3, 3) cable crosses in length. Work incs into cable patt.

CO 2 sts at each end of next 2 rows—42 (53, 64) sts.

Body: Change to dpns, work 1 row, and CO 24 sts between the sides—66 (77, 88) sts; you will have 6 (7, 8) cables around. Pm before cable nearest right leg to mark beg of rnd. Work in cable patt as established for 2 cable crossings in length plus 3 rnds.

Leg openings: Work to 1 st before beg of rnd, BO 8 sts in following patt (P1, K6, P1), work next 13 sts, BO 8 sts in following patt (P1, K6, P1), finish rnd.

On next rnd, work in cable patt as established, and CO 8 sts over BO sts—66 (77, 88) sts.

Cont in cable patt for 1 (1, 2) cable crossings in length plus 3 rnds, and AT THE SAME TIME dec over each leg opening on every other rnd as follows:

1st dec: P1, K2tog, K2, K2tog, P1.

2nd dec: P1, K2tog, K2tog, P1.

3rd dec: P1, P2tog, P1.

4th dec: P1, P2tog.

5th dec: P2tog.

Now there is only 1 purl st instead of a cable.

Roll collar: Work in K1, P1 ribbing, with a dec of K2tog over each cable and P2tog on each side of cable around—36 (44, 52) sts. Cont in ribbing for 4¾" and then BO in ribbing.

Leg bands: PU 20 sts around the leg opening and work 12 rnds in K1, P1 ribbing. BO in ribbing. Work other leg the same way.

Finishing: Fold down collar on RS.

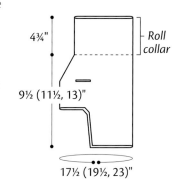

4¾"

Roll collar

9½ (11½, 13)"

17½ (19½, 23)"

"So! Here we are, the cutest dogs in town."

raglan sweater

SIZES

S (M, L)

FINISHED MEASUREMENTS

Circumference: 16 (19½, 23½)"

Length: 10¼ (11½, 13½)" excluding roll collar

MATERIALS

Bulky-weight 100% wool (5)

MC   100 (200, 200) g; 110 (220, 220) yds

CC   100 g; 110 yds

Needles: Set of size 15 (10 mm) double-pointed needles or size required for gauge

4 stitch markers

2 stitch holders

GAUGE

10 sts and 16 rnds = 4" in ribbing unstretched

INSTRUCTIONS

Back: With MC, CO 30 (40, 50) sts; join, being careful not to twist sts, pm. Work 5 rnds in K1, P1 ribbing.

Cont in St st as follows:

Rnd 1: Knit.

Rnd 2: [Inc 1, K6 (8, 10)] around—35 (45, 55) sts.

Rnd 3: Change to CC and knit around.

Rnd 4: Change to MC, [inc 1, K7 (9, 11)] around—40 (50, 60) sts.

Rnds 5 to 8: Knit.

Cont in stripe patt alternating 1 rnd CC and 5 rnds MC, until piece measures about 6 (6¾, 7½)", ending with 2 (4, 2) rnds MC.

Leg openings: Work to 2 sts before beg of rnd. BO 4, work 12 (17, 22) sts, BO 4, finish rnd—13 (18, 23) sts for front and 19 (24, 29) sts for back, put sts on holders. Cut yarn and set piece aside.

Legs: With MC, CO 19 (21, 23) sts. Using two dpns, work back and forth in P1 (K1, P1) ribbing for 5 rows. Work 2 rows in St st. Cont stripe patt until piece measures about 2¾ (3½, 4¼)", ending with 2 (4, 2) rows MC. Note that when there is only 1 row CC, slide sts to the other end of needle so you can pick up the working yarn. BO 2 sts at beg and end of next row. Place rem 15 (17, 19) sts on holder. Work other leg the same way.

Raglan shaping: Work sts from holders as follows: front, pm, first leg, pm, back, pm, second leg, pm—62 (76, 90) sts. Join, and work in the rnd, dec for raglan shaping at each marker as follows: K1, sl1-K1-psso, (work to 3 sts before next marker, K2tog, K2, sl1-K1-psso) until 3 sts rem, end K2tog, K1—8 sts dec—54 (68, 82) sts rem. Dec on every 4th (3rd, 3rd) rnd until 30 (36, 42) sts rem.

Roll collar: With MC, work in K1, P1 ribbing until collar measures 4¾". BO loosely in ribbing.

Finishing: Sew leg seams. Fold down collar on RS.

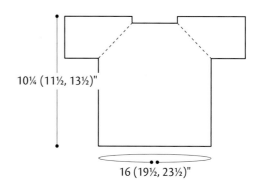

10¼ (11½, 13½)"

16 (19½, 23½)"

bandana

FINISHED MEASUREMENTS

27½" wide x 7" long

MATERIALS

1 skein of Silk Garden from Noro (45% silk, 45% kid mohair, 10% wool; 50 g; 109 yds) 〖4〗

Needles: Size 10½ (6.5 mm) or size required for gauge

Crochet hook: Size H/8 (5 mm)

GAUGE: 14 sts and 28 rows = 4" in garter st

INSTRUCTIONS

CO 4 sts and knit 1 row.

Work in garter st and CO 2 new sts with backward loop (see page 60) at end of every row until there are 96 sts total. BO loosely but do not cut yarn.

Work crab st (see page 60) along the edges of the two diagonal sides (about 10 sts for every 4").

chew ring

FINISHED MEASUREMENT

Circumference: Approx 19¾"

MATERIALS

50 g bulky-weight hemp 〖5〗

Crochet hook: Size L/11 (8 mm)

INSTRUCTIONS

Ch 30 and join into a ring with a sl st. Ch 1, work 1 sc into each ch by working under 2 loops of the ch. Join with 1 sl st. Work in yarn tails securely.

"Don't we look stunning in our colorful bandanas?"

"Let's play! The ring is crocheted with a thick hemp yarn so it's great to bite on."

41

"My coat is super easy to get on and off because it zips up the back."

42

zippered coat

SIZES

S (M, L)

FINISHED MEASUREMENTS

Circumference:
17¼ (20½, 23½)"

Length to beg of rolled collar: 13¾ (16¼, 18½)"

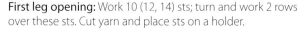

MATERIALS

200 (300, 400) g; 220 (330, 440) yds of bulky-weight 100% wool (5)

Needles: Size 10½ (6.5 mm) and size 11 (8 mm) or size required for gauge

Separating zipper 12 (16, 18)" long

2 stitch markers

1 stitch holder

GAUGE

13 sts and 22 rows = 4" in seed st on smaller needles

Seed stitch

Row 1: (K1, P1) across.

Row 2: Knit the purl sts and purl the knits sts as they face you.

INSTRUCTIONS

Back: With smaller needles, CO 45 (53, 59) sts and work in seed st until piece measures 4¾ (6, 7)". End with a WS row.

On next row, work until 3 sts rem, K2tog, P1. Work decs in seed st on EOR a total of 2 (3, 4) times. End with a WS row.

First leg opening: Work 10 (12, 14) sts; turn and work 2 rows over these sts. Cut yarn and place sts on a holder.

BO 3 sts and finish row, working decs as set. Work 7 rows over these sts. End at leg opening. CO 3 sts over the BO sts and work sts from holder—39 (46, 51) sts total. Cont dec until 37 (41, 45) sts rem; pm at each end to mark center of coat/stomach.

Work other side the same way, reversing shaping by inc 1 st on the same end as the decs on EOR until there are 39 (46, 51) sts. End on a WS row.

Second leg opening: Work as for first leg opening. Cont incs until there are 45 (53, 59) sts.

Work without shaping for 4¾ (6, 7)", ending on a WS row. BO kw.

Roll collar: With larger needles and RS facing, PU 39 (45, 53) sts. Work in P1, (K1, P1) ribbing until collar is 6¼" long. BO in ribbing.

Finishing: Sew zipper at back and then sew seam of rest of piece up to collar. Seam collar with WS facing tog because it will be folded down.

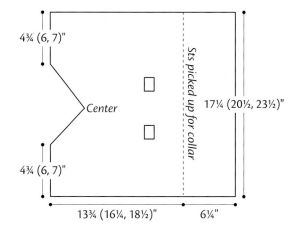

norwegian sweater

SIZES

S (M, L)

FINISHED MEASUREMENTS

Circumference: 17½ (19½, 23)"

Length: 11¾ (13¾, 15¾)" excluding roll collar

MATERIALS

Hauk (100% wool treated with Teflon) from Dale of Norway

100 (100, 150) g; 228 (228, 342) yds in color Light Gray

50 g; 114 yds in color Natural White

50 g; 114 yds in color Charcoal Gray

Needles: Size 6 (4 mm) straight and a set of size 6 (4 mm) double-pointed needles or size required for gauge

3 stitch markers

2 stitch holders

GAUGE

22 sts and 25 rnds = 4" in St st

INSTRUCTIONS

Charts 1, 2, and 3 are on page 48.

Back: With light gray, CO 49 (55, 63) sts and purl 1 row. Work in lice patt (chart 1) and AT THE SAME TIME CO 2 sts at beg of every row 12 (14, 16) times —73 (83, 95) sts.

Cont in lice patt, inc 1 st at each side on EOR until there are 89 (99, 111) sts. Pm in 45th (50th, 56th) st to mark center back.

Body: CO 9 (13, 15) sts at end of row—98 (112, 126) sts. Change to dpns and join to work in the rnd, pm. Cont in lice patt until piece measures 4¼ (5¼, 6)". Work star patt (chart 2) with natural white. Knit 3 rnds with light gray.

Leg openings: Count off 15 (19, 21) sts at center for stomach and place 8 (10, 12) sts at each side on a holder.

Stomach: Work 8 rows of chart 3 over 15 (19, 21) sts for stomach, beg with 1 (3, 4) sts in light gray.

Back: Work 8 rows of chart 3 over the rem 67 (73, 81) sts, beg with 3 (3, 5) sts in light gray.

On next rnd, work across stomach sts, CO 6 (8, 10) sts over leg opening, work across back sts, CO 6 (8, 10) sts over leg opening—94 (108, 122) sts. Join, pm, and dec 4 (0, 2) sts evenly spaced on next rnd—90 (108, 120) sts.

Cont chart 3 and work decs as follows:

Dec on rnd 14: *K13 (16, 18) sts, K2tog; rep from * 6 times—84 (102, 114) sts.

Dec on rnd 20: *K12 (15, 17) sts, K2tog; rep from * 6 times—78 (96, 108) sts.

Complete chart 3.

With light gray, work in St st until piece measures 4 (4¼, 4¾)" from leg opening.

Roll collar: Work in K1, P1 ribbing until collar is 3¼" long. BO in ribbing.

Ribbed edging: With light gray, pick up and knit sts along back and stomach edge (20 sts for every 4") and work around in K1, P1 ribbing on dpns for ⅝". BO in ribbing.

Leg bands: Work 8 (10, 12) sts from st holder in ribbing and PU 24 (26, 28) sts around leg opening in ribbing. Work in K1, P1 ribbing for 2". BO in ribbing. Work other leg same way.

Finishing: Fold down collar and fold up legs on RS.

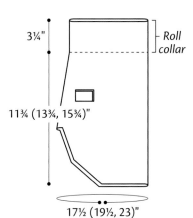

3¼"

Roll collar

11¾ (13¾, 15¾)"

17½ (19½, 23)"

"What about these coats?!
We certainly brighten up
the streets when we are
out and about."

overcoat WITH spots OR blocks

SIZES

S/M (M/L)

FINISHED MEASUREMENTS

Before felting:

Circumference: 7 (9) spots/blocks = 15 (18¼)"

Length: 12 (14) spots/blocks = 21¼ (24¾)"

After felting:

Circumference: 7 (9) spots/blocks = 11¾ (14½)"

Length: 12 (14) spots/blocks = 15½ (18¼)"

MATERIALS

Worsted-weight 100% wool (4)

MC 100 g; 218 yds in color Black

CC 50 (100) g; 109 (218) yds in color Multi

Needles: Size 10½ (6.5 mm) or size required for gauge

10"-long piece of Velcro

Sharp needle and sewing thread

GAUGE

14 sts and 23 rows = 4" before felting

Intarsia: You'll need about 2 yards of yarn for each spot and 2½ yards for each block. Make a yarn butterfly or bobbin for each spot/ block. Twist yarns around each other on WS when changing yarns. After each color change, knot the two ends or splice them.

INSTRUCTIONS

Charts for blocks and spots are on page 48.

Back: With MC, CO 42 (54) sts and purl 1 row.

Work in St st with MC and CC following either chart for blocks or spots for 9 rows.

Inc 1 st at each side and then on every 10th row until there are 50 (66) sts.

Work without further shaping until there are a total of 51 (71) rows.

Stomach straps: With MC, CO 25 (30) sts at each side—92 (114) sts. Work following same chart as before, working the newly CO sts with MC, or incorporating a few more motifs into beg of stomach straps if desired. Work to 84 (105) rows. BO 24 (29) sts at each side and then dec 1 st at each side on every row until 42 (54) sts rem.

Cont without further shaping until there are a total of 100 (120) rows.

Neck straps: With MC, CO 15 (20) sts at each side—72 (94) sts. Follow the same chart as before and work the newly CO sts with MC only. Beg decs on next row as follows: Work 15 (20) sts, pm, dec 1 st, work to last 17 (22) sts, dec 1 st, pm, work 15 (20) sts. Work decs on every other row until 30 (42) sts rem between markers— total of 60 (82) sts. Cont without shaping until there are a total of 120 (140) rows. BO in color patt.

Felting: Machine wash the coat in hot water with a little soap. Check progress often and remove when desired size. Smooth coat after washing, and then lay flat to dry.

Finishing: Cut the Velcro into pieces to fit stomach and neck straps. Sew Velcro pieces (the side with the "barbs") securely to WS of the straps on one side of the coat, and then sew the other side of the Velcro on the RS of the straps on the other side of the coat so that the coat fits comfortably around the dog's stomach and neck.

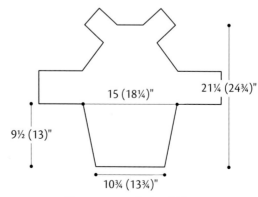

Measurements before felting

15 (18¼)"

21¼ (24¾)"

9½ (13)"

10¾ (13¾)"

Norwegian Sweater

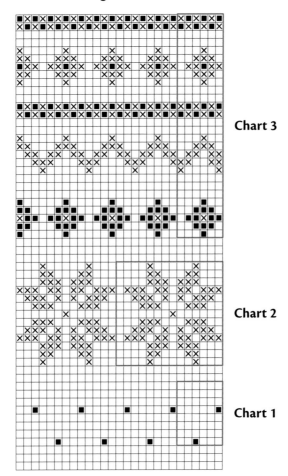

Chart 3

Chart 2

Chart 1

Key
☐ Light gray
☒ Natural white
■ Charcoal gray

Overcoat with Spots or Blocks

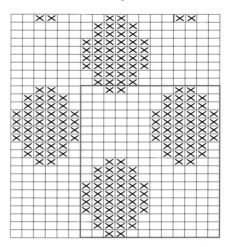

Chart for Spots

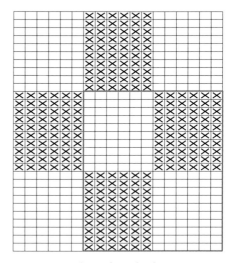

Chart for Blocks

Key
☐ A
☒ B

MATERIALS

1 skein of of Silk Garden from Noro (45% silk, 45% kid mohair, 10% wool; 50 g; 110 yds) (**4**)

Needles: Two size 8 (5 mm) double-pointed needles for I-cord

59"-long nylon cord, ⅝" in diameter for leash

Carabiner hook, ¾" wide

Purchased collar, ⅝" wide

INSTRUCTIONS

Collar

CO 7 sts onto a dpn. Purl 1 row, knit 1 row. Do not turn; instead slide sts to other end of needle, pull yarn, and knit across (I-cord). Work for 1" or length from latch to D-ring on purchased collar. K2, BO 2, knit rem sts.

On next row, CO 2 new sts over the BO sts. Now cont I-cord until it is long enough to cover purchased collar. BO sts.

Pull the purchased collar through the I-cord, making sure that the D-ring is free, and sew securely on each side.

"I can tell that people are looking at me. Of course, because I have my finest leash on today."

Leash

CO 7 sts onto a dpn. Purl 1 row, knit 1 row. Do not turn; instead slide sts to other end of needle, pull yarn, and knit across (I-cord). Work I-cord until leash is 59" long. BO sts.

Pull the nylon cord through the I-cord and sew securely at each end.

Fold one end down 8" and sew. Sew the carabiner hook securely to the other end.

Optional: Make a flower (see page 28) and attach to one end of collar.

SIZES

S (M, L)

FINISHED MEASUREMENTS

Circumference: 16 (19½, 23½)"

Length: 13¾ (15¾, 17¾)"

MATERIALS

150 (200, 250) g; 250 (330, 670) yds of bulky-weight wool/acrylic blend (5)

Crochet hook: Size H/8 (5 mm) or size required for gauge

One "doggie" button

GAUGE

12 sts and 16 rows = 4" in sc

INSTRUCTIONS

Turn and ch 1 at end of every row.

Back: Ch 20 (26, 30).

Work in single crochet, inc 1 st at each side on every other row until there are 36 (46, 54) sts.

Body: On next row, ch 4 new sts at each side—44 (54, 62) sts. Inc 1 st on EOR until there are 48 (62, 72) sts.

Crochet without further shaping until piece measures 8¼ (9¾, 11¾)".

Leg openings: Sc 6 (8, 10); turn with ch 1, and work 4 rows over these sts. Cut yarn. Sk 8 (9, 10) sts and sc 20 (28, 32); turn and work 4 rows over these sts. Cut yarn. Sk 8 (9, 10) sts and sc in the last 6 (8, 10) sts; turn and work 4 rows over these sts.

Joining row: On next row, sc across all sts and ch 5 (5, 6) over each leg opening—42 (54, 64) sts. Dec 1 st over each leg opening on every 4th row 4 times. AT THE SAME TIME at 1½ (2, 2)" above top leg opening, make a facing at the right edge for the button.

Facing: Ch 3 at right edge; turn with ch 1. Work 5 rows across all sts.

Buttonhole: On next row, at left edge (opposite the facing), sc 2, ch 2, sk 2 sts, finish row.

Crochet 3 rows.

Collar: Work across row until 7 sts rem on right edge, 1 sl st; turn with ch 1 and work 1 sl st in the 2nd st from previous row, sc until 4 sts rem, 1 sl st, turn with ch 1. *Work 1 sl st in 2nd st from previous row, sc until 2 sts rem before last turn, 1 sl st; turn with ch 1.* Rep from * to * until you've turned 3 (4, 5) times at each side.

Finishing: Sew stomach seam of jacket right sides tog up to facing. Sew down facing on WS. Sew button on top of sewn facing through both layers.

With RS facing, work 1 rnd of sc around edge of body and leg openings. With WS facing, work 1 row sc along facing and collar.

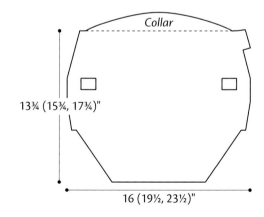

Collar

13¾ (15¾, 17¾)"

16 (19½, 23½)"

"I look my best in this stylish jacket. The front opening is closed with a cute little doggie button."

FINISHED MEASUREMENTS

Approx 19¾" x 21¾"

MATERIALS

Bulky-weight 100% wool **5**

MC   500 g; 546 yds in color Gray

CC   100 g; 109 yds in color Burgundy

Needles: Size 19 (15 mm) circular (32") or size required for gauge

GAUGE

12 sts and 20 rows = 4" in St st with 2 strands of yarn held tog as one

Double Knitting Pattern

Worked over even number of sts.

Double knitting is a technique that allows you to make two layers (a front and a back) of knitted fabric at the same time. You will cast on a total of 60 stitches, and as you work the pattern

30 stitches will form one layer and the alternating 30 stitches will form the other layer. The pattern is worked by alternating slipped stitches and knit stitches, and is repeated on every row. An easy way to remember the pattern is to look at the stitches that face you: if it's a knit stitch, then knit it, and if it's a purl stitch, then slip it purlwise with yarn in front. The square motif is created by attaching burgundy yarn in the middle of a row and working several stitches in burgundy for 8 rows.

Every row: (Sl 1 pw wyif, K1) across.

INSTRUCTIONS

With two strands of gray held tog, CO 60 sts. Cont with 2 strands held tog and work back and forth in double knitting patt for 48 rows.

Burgundy block: Work 27 sts in patt with gray, attach 2 strands of burgundy and hold tog (leaving a long tail), work next 7 sts with burgundy (keeping both gray and burgundy in front when slipping a st), finish row with gray. On next row, work 25 sts with gray, work next 7 sts with burgundy, finish row with gray. Rep these 2 rows a total of 4 times. Cut burgundy after 8th row.

With gray, work in patt for 48 rows.

BO in K1, P1 ribbing.

Finishing: Lay the rug out flat and use long tail from burgundy to sew around the burgundy block through both layers.

striped food mat

FINISHED MEASUREMENTS

Before felting: Approx 19¾" x 24¾"

After felting: Approx 15¾" x 22"

MATERIALS

Bulky-weight 100% wool (5)

  200 g; 218 yds in color White

  200 g; 218 yds in color Black

Needles: Size 10½ (6.5 mm) circular (32") or size required for gauge

GAUGE

12 sts and 24 rows = 4" before felting

INSTRUCTIONS

Bottom corner: With black, CO 2 sts and work in garter st stripes as follows. Carry yarn not in use loosely up side.

Row 1 (black): K1f&b in first st, K1—3 sts.

Row 2 (white): K1, K1f&b in next st, K1—4 sts.

Row 3 (white): K1, K1f&b in next st, knit across—5 sts.

Row 4 (black): K1, K1f&b in next st, knit across—6 sts.

Row 5 (black): K1, K1f&b in next st, knit across—7 sts.

Cont 2-row stripes and work incs as established until there are 84 sts (approx 19¾" along straight side).

Straight sides: Cont 2-row stripes, work K1, K2tog tbl at beg of even-numbered rows and K1, K1f&b at beg of odd-numbered rows. Work until piece measures approx 24¾" on longest side.

Top corner: Cont 2-row stripes, and from now on, dec at beg of every row by working, K1, K2tog tbl, knit across. Cont decs until 2 sts rem. BO all sts.

Felting: Machine wash the mat in hot water with a little soap. Check progress frequently and remove when desired size. Smooth out mat and let dry completely.

"It's so cozy and soft here. I can really snuggle up in this big blanket."

patchwork blanket

FINISHED MEASUREMENTS

Approx 47¼" x 47¼"

MATERIALS

1200 g; 1300 yds of bulky-weight 100% wool **5**

Needles: Size 13 (9 mm) circular (32") or size required for gauge

Cable needle

GAUGE

12 sts and 17 rows = 4" in seed st

Seed Stitch

Row 1: (P1, K1) across.

Row 2 and all following rows: Knit the purl sts and purl the knit sts as they face you.

INSTRUCTIONS

CO 149 sts and work back and forth on circular needle.

First patt: Set up patt as follows: K1 (edge st), (work 21 seed sts, work 21 sts following chart) 3 times, work 21 seed sts, K1 (edge st). Work through 28 rows of chart.

Second patt: Set up patt as follows: P1 (edge st), (work 21 sts following chart, work 21 seed sts) 3 times, work 21 sts following chart, P1 (edge st). Work through 28 rows of chart.

Rep these 56 rows of first and second patt a total of 3 times—168 rows total.

Work the 28 rows of first patt once more—196 rows total.

BO kw on chart sts and in seed st over seed sts.

Finishing: Steam press blanket on WS.

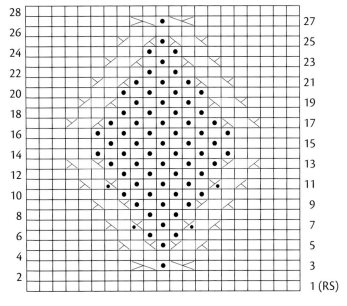

Key

- ☐ K on RS, P on WS
- ⊡ P on RS, K on WS
- 2/1CFP: sl 2 sts to cn and hold at front, P1, K2 from cn
- 1/2CBP: sl 1 st to cn and hold at back, K2, P1 from cn
- 3/2CFP: sl 3 sts to cn and hold at front, K2, (P1, K2) from cn
- 2/1CF: sl 1 sts to cn and hold at front, K1, K2 from cn
- 1/2CB: sl 1 st to cn and hold at back, K2, K1 from cn

round crocheted pillow

FINISHED MEASUREMENTS

Before felting: Approx 31½" in diameter

After felting: Approx 27½" in diameter

MATERIALS

Bulky-weight 100% wool (**5**)

- **MC** 400 g; 435 yds in color Blue
- **CC** 350 g; 380 yds in color Green

Crochet hook: Size J/10 (6 mm)

Round pillow form, approx 27½" diameter

INSTRUCTIONS

Half Double Crochet Variation

This pattern of half double crochet (hdc) uses the loop behind the 2 loops that one usually crochets into.

Rnd 1: Wrap yarn around hook, insert hook into next st, wrap yarn around and bring through (3 loops on hook), wrap yarn around hook and draw through all 3 loops.

Rnd 2 and all following rnds: Work half double crochet in the loop behind the 2 loops so that you have a twisted ridge that resembles knit sts.

Striped Side

With blue, ch 4 and join into a ring with sl st.

Rnd 1: Ch 1, 10 sc in ring, sl st into first st of rnd.

Rnd 2: Change to green and ch 2, 2 hdc in each sc around, end with sl st in beg ch loop—20 sts.

From this point on, work pillow in rnd 2 of hdc variation above, and inc as indicated.

Rnd 3: Change to blue and ch 2, (2 hdc in next st, 1 hdc in next st) around 30 sts.

Change color at beg of each new rnd and beg with ch 2. End each rnd with sl st in beg ch loop.

Rnd 4: (Hdc 2 in next st, 1 hdc in the next 2 sts) around—40 sts.

Rnd 5: (Hdc 2 in next st, 1 hdc in next 3 sts) around—50 sts.

Cont inc on every rnd, with 1 more st between incs. Incs should stack one above the other.

Work until there are 34 sts between incs—350 sts, approx 31½" in diameter.

Star Side

With blue, ch 4 and join into a ring with sl st.

Rnd 1: Ch 1, 7 sc in ring, sl st in first st of rnd, ch 1.

The first blue ch st on rnd counts as 1 st.

Rnd 2: Change to green and work 1 sc in first st of previous rnd, (1 sc with blue and 1 sc with green in next st) a total of 6 times, sk 1 st, sl st with blue into ch from previous rnd, ch 1—14 sts.

From this point on, work sc into back loops only.

Rnd 3: Sc 2 with green into blue st, (1 sc blue into green st, 2 sc green into blue st) a total of 6 times, sk 1 st, sl st with blue into ch of previous rnd, ch 1—21 sts.

The first blue ch st on the rnd counts as 1 st.

Rnd 4: Sc 2 with green into blue st, 1 sc green into green st, (1 sc blue into green st, 2 sc green into blue st, 1 sc green into green st) a total of 6 times, skip 1 st, sl st with blue into ch of previous rnd, ch 1—28 sts.

Rnd 5: Sc 2 green into blue st, 2 sc green, (1 sc blue, 2 sc green into next st, 2 sc green) a total of 6 times, sk 1 st, sl st with blue into ch of previous rnd, ch 1—35 sts.

Note: Catch the blue yarn at the "points" so that there won't be long strands on WS.

Cont as established, with 1 more green st in each group until there are 20 green sts in each group. Note that strands on WS should be very loose—they will fill in during felting.

Rnd 22: Sc 2 blue into same first blue ch of rnd, 19 sc green, (1 sc blue in next green st, 2 sc blue in next blue st, 19 sc green) a total of 6 times, sk 1 st, sl st with blue into first ch on rnd, ch 1.

Rnd 23: Sc 2 blue in same first blue ch of rnd, 2 sc blue, 18 sc green, (1 sc blue in next green st, 2 sc blue into next blue st, 2 sc blue, 18 sc green) a total of 6 times, sk 1 st, sl st with blue into first ch of rnd, ch 1.

Rnd 24: Sc 2 sc blue into same first blue ch of rnd, 4 sc blue, 17 sc green, (1 sc blue into next green st, 2 sc blue into next blue st, 4 sc blue, 17 sc green) a total of 6 times, sk 1 st, sl st with blue into first ch of rnd, ch 1.

Cont as established, with 1 less green in each group until there are no more green sts, *and* cont inc 7 sts per rnd as before until there are 49 sts between incs—350 sts, approx 31½" in diameter.

Felting: Machine wash both sides in hot water with a little soap. Check progress frequently and remove when desired size. Shape sides to correct measurements and let dry completely.

With RS facing out, join the two sides tog with blanket stitch (see page 61), leaving an opening; insert pillow form, and then finish seaming.

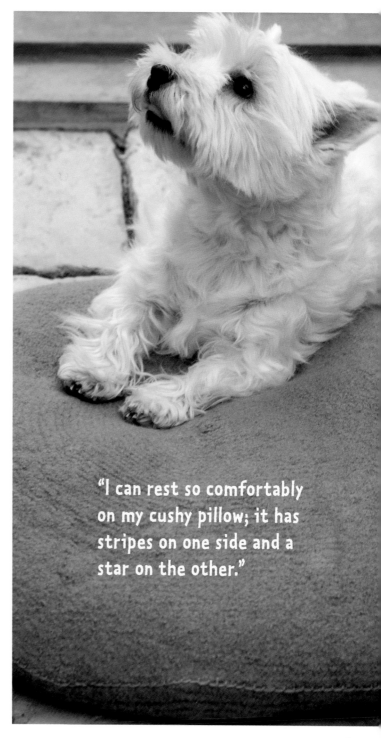

"I can rest so comfortably on my cushy pillow; it has stripes on one side and a star on the other."

"I've played all day and gotten very tired. So, it's very nice to lie on my large, soft pillow and dream about juicy bones."

square knitted pillow

FINISHED MEASUREMENTS

Approx 25½" x 25½"

MATERIALS

Bulky-weight cotton/acrylic blend (5)

    250 g; 435 yds in color Pink

    250 g; 435 yds in color Multi

    50 g; 87 yds in color Brown

    50 g; 87 yds in color Beige

Needles: Size 10 (6 mm) or size required for gauge

Crochet hook: Size J/10 (6 mm)

Pillow form, 27½" x 27½"

GAUGE

15 sts and 22 rows = 4" in St st

INSTRUCTIONS

Side 1: With pink, CO 96 sts and work in St st until piece measures 24¾". BO all sts. With brown and tapestry needle, use duplicate st (see page 61) to embroider the motif from the chart in the middle of the piece.

Side 2: With multicolored yarn, work as for side 1.

Edging: With beige, work 1 rnd of sc around edge of each piece. With RS facing out, crochet pieces tog with sc, adding an extra st at each corner. Don't forget to insert the pillow form before you finish crocheting the pieces tog.

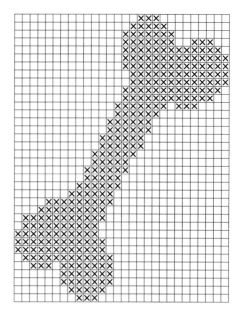

Key

☐ Multi

☒ Brown

In this section, you'll find a brief explanation for some of the techniques used in the projects in this book.

Backward Loop Cast On: With the yarn from the needle coming around the back of the thumb to the front, insert the needle under the yarn on the front side of the thumb. Release the yarn from the thumb and tighten the loop gently. Repeat for the required number of stitches.

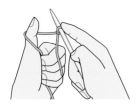

Cable Cast On: Insert the right-hand needle between two stitches on the left-hand needle and knit a stitch. Place the new stitch on the left-hand needle. Repeat for the required number of stitches.

Chain (ch): Make a slipknot over the hook. Insert the hook through the loop and tighten the yarn slightly. Wrap the yarn around the hook and bring it through the loop. Continue bringing the yarn through each loop until the chain has the required number of stitches. Do not count the loop of the slipknot.

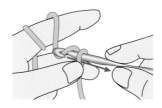

Crab Stitch: Also known as reverse single crochet because it is worked from left to right instead of from right to left. When you get to the end of the row, chain one, do not turn; *insert the hook into the stitch at the right, yarn over the hook, draw through a loop, yarn over the hook, and draw through two loops on the hook. Repeat from * across the row. Fasten off.

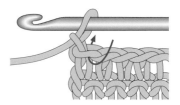

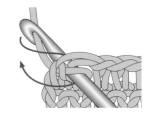

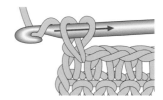

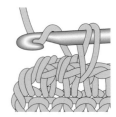

Double Crochet (dc): Wrap the yarn around the hook and insert the hook into the specified chain or stitch.

Wrap the yarn around the hook and pull it through the stitch; (wrap the yarn around the hook and pull the hook through two loops on hook) twice. Continue in this way across the row. Turn and chain three.

The next row begins in the stitch next to the one below the turning chain and ends with a stitch in the top of the turning chain, unless otherwise instructed.

Duplicate Stitch: This method of embroidery "duplicates" a knit stitch, which makes a motif appear as if it was knit into the knitting. It can be done horizontally and vertically.

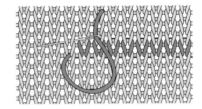

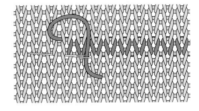

Horizontal duplicate stitch

Vertical duplicate stitch

Half Double Crochet (hdc): * Wrap the yarn around the hook, insert the hook into the chain or stitch indicated. Wrap the yarn around the hook and pull it through the stitch (three loops remain on the hook).

Wrap the yarn around the hook and pull it through all three loops on the hook. Repeat from * for the required number of stitches.

Knit 1 in Stitch Below: Insert the right-hand needle into the stitch below the first stitch on the left-hand needle, and knit it in the normal manner. Drop the stitch above from the needle.

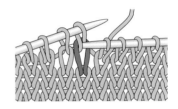

Joining Pieces with a Blanket Stitch: The two sides of the Crocheted Pillow on page 56 are joined with a blanket stitch along the edges. Thread yarn onto a tapestry needle. With right sides of the pieces facing out, secure the yarn at the edge of the bottom piece. Insert the needle through one stitch on the front piece and through the corresponding stitch on the back piece; then pull the yarn through, making sure the yarn is under the needle. Continue working from left to right all around, trying to keep the stitches evenly spaced apart.

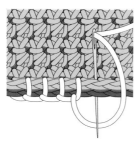

Single Crochet (sc): Insert the hook into the specified chain or stitch, wrap the yarn around the hook, and pull it through the stitch; wrap the yarn around the hook and pull it through two loops on the hook. Continue in this way across the row. Turn and chain one.

The next row begins in the first stitch after the turning chain and ends on the last stitch.

Single Crochet Decrease (dec): (Insert the hook into the next stitch, yarn over, pull up a loop) twice; yarn over and pull through all three loops on the hook.

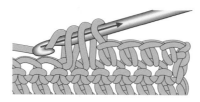

Single Crochet Increase (inc): Work two single crochet stitches into the same stitch.

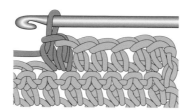

Slip Stitch (sl st): Insert the hook into the specified stitch, wrap the yarn around the hook, and pull it through both loops on the hook.

Working into Crochet Loops: Normally stitches are worked into both loops of a crochet stitch on the row below. However, some patterns will instruct you to work into the front loops or back loops only.

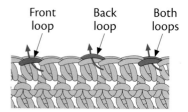

Front loop   Back loop   Both loops

abbreviations AND glossary

approx	approximately		**oz**	ounce(s)
beg	begin(ning)		**P**	purl
BO	bind off		**P2tog**	purl 2 stitches together—1 stitch decreased
ch	chain(s) or chain stitch(es)		**patt**	pattern(s)
CC	contrasting color		**pm**	place marker
cn	cable needle		**psso**	pass slipped stitch over
CO	cast on		**PU**	pick up and knit
cont	continue(ing)(s)		**pw**	purlwise
dc	double crochet(s)		**rem**	remain(ing)
dec(s)	decrease(ing)(s)		**rep**	repeat(s)
dpn(s)	double-pointed needle(s)		**RH**	right hand
EOR	every other row		**rnd(s)**	round(s)
est	established		**RS**	right side
g	gram(s)		**sc**	single crochet(s)
garter st	garter stitch: back and forth, knit every row; in the rnd, knit 1 rnd, purl 1 rnd		**sc2tog**	single crochet 2 stitches together—1 stitch decreased
hdc	half double crochet(s)		**sk**	skip
inc(s)	increase(ing)(s)		**sl1-K1-psso**	slip 1 stitch knitwise, knit 1 stitch, pass slipped stitch over knit stitch—1 stitch decreased
K	knit			
K1f&b	knit into front and back of same stitch—1 stitch increased		**sl st**	slip stitch(es)
			sp	space
K1tbl	knit 1 stitch through back loop		**st(s)**	stitch(es)
K2tog	knit 2 stitches together—1 stitch decreased		**St st**	Stockinette stitch: back and forth, knit 1 row, purl 1 row; knit in the round, knit every round
kw	knitwise			
m	meter(s)		**tbl**	through back loop(s)
M1	make 1 stitch: lift strand between two sts and knit into back loop—1 stitch increased		**tog**	together
			WS	wrong side
MC	main color		**wyif**	with yarn in front
mm	millimeter(s)		**yd(s)**	yard(s)
			YO	yarn over(s)

Use the following tables as a guideline to help you find suitable yarns.

KNITTING STANDARD YARN-WEIGHT SYSTEM

Yarn-Weight Symbol and Category Names	1 SUPER FINE	2 FINE	3 LIGHT	4 MEDIUM	5 BULKY	6 SUPER BULKY
Types of Yarns in Category	Sock, Fingering, Baby	Sport, Baby	DK, Light Worsted	Worsted, Afghan, Aran	Chunky, Craft, Rug	Bulky, Roving
Knit Gauge Ranges in Stockinette Stitch to 4"	27 to 32 sts	23 to 26 sts	21 to 24 sts	16 to 20 sts	12 to 15 sts	6 to 11 sts
Recommended Needle in U.S. Size Range	1 to 3	3 to 5	5 to 7	7 to 9	9 to 11	11 and larger
Recommended Needle in Metric Size Range	2.25 to 3.25 mm	3.25 to 3.75 mm	3.75 to 4.5 mm	4.5 to 5.5 mm	5.5 to 8 mm	8 mm and larger

CROCHETING STANDARD YARN-WEIGHT SYSTEM

Yarn-Weight Symbol and Category Names	1 SUPER FINE	2 FINE	3 LIGHT	4 MEDIUM	5 BULKY	6 SUPER BULKY
Types of Yarns in Category	Sock, Fingering, Baby	Sport, Baby	DK, Light Worsted	Worsted, Afghan, Aran	Chunky, Craft, Rug	Bulky, Roving
Crochet Gauge Ranges in Single Crochet to 4"	21 to 32 sts	16 to 20 sts	12 to 17 sts	11 to 14 sts	8 to 11 sts	5 to 9 sts
Recommended Hook in U.S. Size Range	B-1 to E-4	E-4 to 7	7 to I-9	I-9 to K-10½	K-10½ to M13	M-13 and larger
Recommended Hook in Metric Size Range	2.25 to 3.5 mm	3.5 to 4.5 mm	4.5 to 5.5 mm	5.5 to 6.5 mm	6.5 to 9 mm	9 mm and larger

METRIC CONVERSIONS

m = yds x 0.9144   g = oz x 28.35

yds = m x 1.0936   oz = g x 0.0352